Sue Graham Mingus

About the Author

HAROLD BLOOM is Sterling Professor of Humanities at Yale University and a former Charles Eliot Norton Professor at Harvard. His more than twenty-five books include *The Best Poems of the English Language: From Chaucer Through Frost*; *Genius*; *How to Read and Why*; *Shakespeare: The Invention of the Human*; *The Western Canon*; *The Book of J*; and *The Anxiety of Influence*. He is a MacArthur Prize Fellow, a member of the American Academy of Arts and Letters, and the recipient of many awards and honorary degrees, including the Academy's Gold Medal for Belles Lettres and Criticism, the International Prize of Catalonia, and the Alfonso Reyes Prize of Mexico.

The Art of
Reading
Poetry

ALSO BY HAROLD BLOOM

The Best Poems of The English Language:
From Chaucer Through Frost (2004)

Hamlet: Poem Unlimited (2003)

Genius: A Mosaic of One Hundred Exemplary Creative Minds (2002)

Stories and Poems for Extremely Intelligent Children of All Ages (2001)

How to Read and Why (2000)

Shakespeare: The Invention of the Human (1998)

Omens of Millennium (1996)

The Western Canon (1994)

The American Religion (1992)

The Book of J (1990)

Ruin the Sacred Truths (1989)

Poetics of Influence (1988)

The Strong Light of the Canonical (1987)

Agon: Towards a Theory of Revisionism (1982)

The Breaking of the Vessels (1982)

The Flight to Lucifer: A Gnostic Fantasy (1979)

Wallace Stevens: The Poems of Our Climate (1977)

Figures of Capable Imagination (1976)

Poetry and Repression (1976)

Kabbalah and Criticism (1975)

A Map of Misreading (1975)

The Anxiety of Influence (1973)

The Ringers in the Tower: Studies in Romantic Tradition (1971)

Yeats (1970)

Commentary to the Poetry and Prose of William Blake (1965)

Blake's Apocalypse (1963)

The Visionary Company (1961)

Shelley's Mythmaking (1959)

The Art of
Reading
Poetry

HAROLD BLOOM

Perennial

An Imprint of HarperCollins*Publishers*

This work is excerpted from *The Best Poems of the English Language: From Chaucer Through Frost* published in hardcover in 2004 by HarperCollins Publishers.

HarperCollins books may be purchased for educational,
business, or sales promotional use.
For information, please e-mail the Special Markets Department
at SPsales@harpercollins.com.

FIRST PERENNIAL EDITION PUBLISHED 2005.

Library of Congress Cataloging-in-Publication Data

Bloom, Harold.
The art of reading poetry / Harold Bloom—1st Perennial ed.
p. cm.
"Excerpted from The best poems of the English Language : from
Chaucer through Frost"—T.p. verso.
ISBN 0-06-076966-1
1. English poetry—History and criticism. 2. American poetry—
History and criticism. I. Bloom, Harold. Best poems of the English
language. II. Title.

PR502.B55 2004
821.009—dc22   2004057292

HB 03.07.2023

The Art of Reading Poetry

I

POETRY essentially is figurative language, concentrated so that its form is both expressive and evocative. Figuration is a departure from the literal, and the form of a great poem itself can be a trope ("turning") or figure. A common dictionary equivalent for "figurative language" is "metaphorical," but a metaphor actually is a highly specific figure, or turning from the literal. Kenneth Burke, a profound student of rhetoric, or the language of figures, distinguished four fundamental tropes: irony, synecdoche, metonymy, and metaphor. As Burke tells us, irony commits those who employ it to issues of presence and absence, since they are saying one thing while meaning something so different that it can be the precise opposite. We learn to wince when Hamlet says: "I humbly thank you" or its equivalent, since the prince generally is neither humble nor grateful.

We now commonly call synecdoche "symbol," since the figurative substitution of a part for a whole also suggests that incompletion in which something within the poem stands for something outside it. Poets frequently identify more with one trope than with the others. Among major American poets, Robert Frost (despite his mass reputation) favors irony, while Walt Whitman is the great master of synecdoche.

In metonymy, contiguity replaces resemblance, since the name or prime aspect of anything is sufficient to indicate it, provided it is near in space to what serves as substitute. Childe Roland, in Browning's remarkable monologue, is represented at the very end by the "slughorn" or trumpet upon which he dauntlessly blows: "Childe Roland to the Dark Tower came."

Metaphor proper transfers the ordinary associations of one word to another, as when Hart Crane beautifully writes "peonies with pony manes," enhancing his metaphor by the pun between "peonies" and "pony." Or again Crane, most intensely metaphorical of poets, refers to the Brooklyn Bridge's curve as its "leap," and then goes on to call the bridge both harp and altar.

Figurations or tropes create meaning, which could not exist without them, and this making of meaning is largest in authentic poetry, where an excess or overflow emanates from figurative language, and brings about a condition of newness. Owen Barfield's *Poetic Diction: A Study in Meaning* is one of the best guides to this process, when he traces part of the poetic history of the English word "ruin."

The Latin verb *ruo,* meaning "rush" or "collapse," led to the substantive *ruina* for what had fallen. Chaucer, equally at home in French and English, helped to domesticate "ruin" as "a falling":

> Min is the ruine of the highe halles,
> The falling of the towers and of the walles.

One feels the chill of that, the voice being Saturn's or time's in "The Knight's Tale." Chaucer's disciple Edmund Spenser has the haunting line:

> The old ruines of a broken tower

My last selection in this book is Hart Crane's magnificent death ode, "The Broken Tower," in which

Spenser's line reverberates. Barfield emphasizes Shakespeare's magnificence in the employment of "ruin," citing "Bare ruin'd choirs where late the sweet birds sang" from Sonnet 73, and the description of Cleopatra's effect upon her lover: "The noble ruin of her magic, Antony." I myself find even stronger the blind Gloucester's piercing outcry when he confronts the mad King Lear (IV, VI, 134–135):

> O ruin'd piece of nature! This great world
> Shall so wear out to nought.

Once Barfield sets one searching, the figurative power of "ruined" seems endless. Worthy of Shakespeare himself is John Donne, in his "A Nocturnal upon St. Lucy's Day," where love resurrects the poet to his ruin:

> Study me then, you who shall lovers be
> At the next world, that is, at the next spring:
>> For I am every dead thing,
>> In whom love wrought new alchemy.
>>> For his art did express
> A quintessence even from nothingness,
> From dull privations, and lean emptiness

He ruined me, and I am re-begot
Of absence, darkness, death; things which are
    not.

Barfield invokes what he rightly calls Milton's "terrific phrase": "Hell saw / Heaven ruining from Heaven," and then traces Wordsworth's allusive return to Milton. Rather than add further instances, I note Barfield's insight, that the figurative power of "ruin" depends upon restoring its original sense of *movement,* of rushing toward a collapse. One of the secrets of poetic rhetoric in English is to romance the etonym (as it were), to renew what Walter Pater called the "finer edges" of words.

2

LANGUAGE, to a considerable extent, is concealed figuration: ironies and synecdoches, metonymies and metaphors that we recognize only when our awareness increases. Real poetry is aware of and exploits these ruined tropes, though it is both a burden and a resource, for later poets in a tradition, that language ages into this wealth of figuration. The major poets of the twentieth century, in Britain and America, were those who could best exploit this equivocal richness: Thomas Hardy, W. B. Yeats, D. H. Lawrence, Robert Frost, T. S. Eliot, Wallace Stevens, and Hart Crane among them.

Eliot professed no use for Walter Pater, who nevertheless haunts his praxis both as poet and as critic, as in the superb "Preludes" from *Prufrock and Other Observations* (1917):

> The conscience of a blackened street
> Impatient to assume the world.
>
> I am moved by fancies that are curled
> Around these images, and cling:
> The notion of some infinitely gentle
> Infinitely suffering thing.

"Assume" goes back to the Latin *assumere,* meaning something like "take," and initially was used in English for receiving a person into association, as when heaven assumed a saint. Over time, "assume" began to mean "to take as being true"; thus Whitman tells his reader: "And what I assume you shall assume." Other meanings include "to put on oneself," as with a garment or insignia, or else "to simulate," a pretending to have. D. H. Lawrence wrote of houses "assuming the sun," perhaps remembering Hamlet's bitter advice to Gertrude: "Assume a virtue, if you have it not."

Eliot's blackened street, "impatient to assume the world," plays, I think, upon both Whitman and Hamlet. Yet the etymology, Pater's "finer edge of words," is renewed: by a dark irony, the street's "conscience" renders it impatient to take up the world even as heaven receives the blessed. "Conscience" comes from Latin *conscientia*, meaning "consciousness," and retains that significance sometimes in Shakespeare, as when the disguised Henry V observes: "I will speak my conscience of the King: I think he would not wish himself anywhere but where he is." Or we can remember Hamlet (as I suspect Eliot does): "Thus conscience doth make cowards of us all," whereas our "conscience" as moral awareness or sense of guilt is later in provenance, and is only secondary to Eliot's lines:

> The conscience of a blackened street
> Impatient to assume the world.

In a sustained, brilliant irony, Eliot imputes consciousness to the street, which in "assume" mistakes itself for heaven. Reflecting on the irony of his images, the poet has a notion of what heaven indeed might "assume": "some infinitely gentle / Infinitely suffering thing." Earlier in "Preludes," Eliot speaks to a waking soul:

> You had such a vision of the street
> As the street hardly understands;

I know nothing better by Eliot than the "Preludes." They so restored the strangeness of meaning that they became immensely fecund. *The Waste Land* founds its style upon them and so, in an intense agon with Eliot, does the lyrical genius of Hart Crane, who fought Eliot's vision yet could not resist Eliot's style and example, the "Preludes" in particular, where urban imagery is raised to an ironic glory.

3

GREATNESS in poetry depends upon splendor of figurative language and on cognitive power, or what Emerson termed "meter-making argument." Shakespeare is first among poets at representing thought, which pragmatically does not differ from *thinking in poetry,* a process not yet fully adumbrated. Angus Fletcher's *Colors of the Mind* can be recommended for its "conjectures on thinking in literature," which is the book's subtitle.

In Shakespeare, thought itself can be considered tragic or comic, or any shade between the two. Or, because of the Shakespearean detachment, so triumphant in the consciousness of Hamlet, we may hear what Wallace Stevens subtly termed "the hum of thoughts evaded in the mind." Clearly, poetic thinking takes place somewhat apart from philosophic thinking. There can be Epicurean poetry, or Platonic literature, in which concepts inform the work of the imagination, but most literary thinking is of a different kind.

Memory is crucial for all thought, but particularly so for poetic thinking. Poetic memory, as Fletcher suggests, allows *recognition,* which he regards as "the central modality of thinking, for literary purposes." "Recognition" here initially is Aristotle's *anagnorisis,* the recognition-scene toward which tragedy quests. Discovery can be a synonym for recognition, in this sense.

One definition of poetic power is that it so fuses thinking and remembering that we cannot separate the two processes. Can a poem, of authentic strength, be composed without remembering a prior poem, whether by the self or by another? Literary thinking relies upon literary memory, and the drama of recognition, in every writer, contains within it a moment of coming to terms with another writer, or with an earlier version of the self. Poetic thinking is contextualized by poetic influences, even in Shakespeare, most gifted of poets, who parodies Marlowe's *Jew of Malta* in *Titus Andronicus,* where Aaron the Moor attempts to overgo in villainy the sublime Barabas, the Marlovian Jew. Shakespeare's *Richard III* is more of an involuntary recollection of Marlowe, and it may be accurate to say that Shakespeare thinks less clearly through Richard III than he does through Aaron. But within two years, in *Richard II,* Shakespeare has so thought through Marlowe's influence (here of *Edward II*) that he audaciously mocks his precursor in what could be called Richard's recognition scene:

> Give me that glass, and therein will I read.
> No deeper wrinkles yet? Hath sorrow struck
> So many blows upon this face of mine
> And made no deeper wounds? O flatt'ring glass,
> Like to my followers in prosperity,

Thou dost beguile me. Was this face the face
That every day under his household roof
Did keep ten thousand men? Was this the face
That like the sun did make beholders wink?
Is this the face which fac'd so many follies,
That was at last out-fac'd by Bolingbroke?
A brittle glory shineth in this face;
As brittle as the glory is the face,
> [*Dashes the glass against the ground.*]
For there it is, crack'd in an hundred shivers.
Mark, silent king, the moral of this sport—
How soon my sorrow hath destroy'd my face.

The delighted audience, most of whom had attended Marlowe's *Dr. Faustus,* would have thrilled to Richard's triple-variant upon Faustus's ecstatic recognition of Helen of Troy, conjured up for him by Mephistopheles:

Was this the face that launched a thousand
ships,
And burnt the topless towers of Ilium?

Here, Shakespearean thought triumphs over influence, as Marlowe returns from the dead, but only in

the colors of Richard II's gorgeous rhetoric. Far sub-
tler, Shakespeare in *The Tempest* gives us his anti-
Faustus, Prospero, whose name is the Italian
translation of the Latin Faustus, each "the favored
one." The recognition scene in matured Shakespeare is
one of a beautifully ironic self-recognition, a splendor
of poetic thinking.

4

THE ART of reading poetry begins with mastering allu-
siveness in particular poems, from the simple to the
very complex. We can start with quite short poems, like
the lyrics of A. E. Housman (1859–1936). Here is his
splendid "Epitaph on an Army of Mercenaries":

> These, in the day when heaven was falling,
>   The hour when earth's foundations fled,
> Followed their mercenary calling
>   And took their wages and are dead.
>
> Their shoulders held the sky suspended;
>   They stood, and earth's foundations stay;
> What God abandoned, these defended,
>   And saved the sum of things for pay.

Housman was a classical scholar, and his ultimate model here might be Simonides, the ancient Greek poet of epitaphs. Elsewhere in Housman, we are advised: "Shoulder the sky my lad, and drink your ale." Richard Wilbur, one of our best contemporary American poets, refers "and took their wages and are dead" to St. Paul's "the wages of sin is death." I think not, and cite instead Shakespeare's superb song from *Cymbeline:*

> Fear no more the heat o' the Sun,
> Nor the furious Winter's rages,
> Thou thy worldly task hast done,
> Home art gone, and ta'en thy wages.
> Golden Lads, and Girls all must,
> As Chimney-Sweepers come to dust.

At issue is how to determine the appropriateness of an allusion, and since great poetry is very nearly as allusive as it is figurative, the question of accuracy in tracing allusiveness is crucial. The echo here is far likelier to be of Shakespeare than of St. Paul, because the mercenaries are hardly being blamed, and the universalism of "Home art gone, and ta'en thy wages" therefore is more appropriate.

Wilbur more usefully finds "the sum of things," fled foundations, and heaven falling in two passages of Book

IV of *Paradise Lost,* where Milton narrates the War in
Heaven between the rebel angels and those who
remain obedient to God:

> . . . horrid confusion leapt
> Upon condition rose: and now all Heav'n
> Had gone to wrack, with ruin overspread,
> Had not th' Almighty Father where he sits
> Shrin'd in his Sanctuary of Heav'n secure,
> Consulting on the sum of things, foreseen
> This tumult . . .
>
> —LINES 668 FF.

> Hell heard the unsufferable noise, Hell saw
> Heav'n ruining from Heav'n, and would have
>   fled
> Affrighted, but strict Fate had cast too deep
> Her dark foundations, and too fast had
>   bound . . .
>
> —LINES 867 FF.

But Housman, no Christian and a good Epicurean,
makes these allusions ironic, since his mercenaries
defended "What God abandoned," unlike the loyal
angels, who followed Christ as he, at God's command,

thrust the fallen angels out of Heaven. So we have a double lesson in allusiveness: is it accurate, and again is it itself figurative, as here?

Recognizing and interpreting allusions depends upon both the reader's learning and her tact. T. S. Eliot, in his charmingly outrageous and frequently unreliable "Notes" to *The Waste Land,* charts some of his allusions while evading others. His famous line—"I will show you fear in a handful of dust"—clearly alludes to the morbid young protagonist of Tennyson's *Maud,* who cries out to us: "And my heart is a handful of dust."

On a vaster scale, all of *The Waste Land,* but particularly Part V, "What the Thunder Said," is endlessly allusive to Walt Whitman's elegy "When Lilacs Last in the Dooryard Bloom'd." From "Lilacs" come Eliot's lilacs and other flowers, his unreal city, his triple self, the "third who always walks beside you," the maternal lamentation, the dead soldiers, and much more, but particularly the song of the hermit-thrush in the pine trees. Eliot's "Notes" refer the hermit-thrush to Chapman's *Handbook of Birdes in Eastern North America,* a somewhat hilarious evasion.

So profuse are the allusions to "Lilacs" in *The Waste Land* that we would forsake credulity to consider them accidental or even "unconscious." Allusion then can be a mode of evasion, or of warding off a precursor. Repressed reference is a defense against overinfluence. As forerunners, Eliot claimed Dante, Baudelaire, the rather minor Jules Laforgue, and Ezra Pound, his friend and mentor, but the authentic father was Walt Whitman, with a strong strain of Tennyson mixed in.

5

ALLUSION is only one strand in the relationship between later and earlier poems. More (in my judgment) than any other kind of imaginative literature, poetry brings its own past alive into its present. There is a benign haunting in poetic tradition, one that transcends the sorrows of influence, particularly the new poet's fear that there is little left for her or him to do. In truth, there is everything remaining to be thought and sung, provided an individual voice is attained.

Poetic voice is immensely difficult to define without examples. I give, almost at random, a sequence of major voices without (at first) identifying them:

1

Ay, but to die, and go we know not where;
To lie in cold obstruction, and to rot;

This sensible warm motion, to become
A kneaded clod; and the delighted spirit
To bathe in fiery floods, or to reside
In thrilling region of thick-ribbed ice;
To be imprison'd in the viewless winds
And blown with restless violence round about
The pendant world; or to be worse than worst
Of those that lawless and incertain thought
Imagine howling—'tis too horrible!
The weariest and most loathed wordly life
That age, ache, penury, and imprisonment
Can lay on nature is a paradise
To what we fear of death.

2

And that must end us, that must be our cure,
To be no more; sad cure; for who would lose,
Though full of pain, this intellectual being,
Those thoughts that wander through eternity,
To perish rather, swallowed up and lost
In the wide womb of uncreated night,
Devoid of sense and motion?

3

Not with more glories, in the ethereal plain,
The sun first rises o'er the purpled main,

Then issuing forth, the rival of his beams
Launched on the bosom of the silver Thames.
Fair nymphs and well-dressed youths around her
    shone,
But every eye was fixed on her alone.
On her white breast a sparkling cross she wore,
Which Jews might kiss, and infidels adore.
Her lively looks a sprightly mind disclose,
Quick as her eyes, and as unfixed as those:
Favours to none, to all she smiles extends,
Oft she rejects, but never once offends.
Bright as the sun, her eyes the gazers strike,
And, like the sun, they shine on all alike.
Yet graceful ease, and sweetness void of pride,
Might hide her faults, if belles had faults to hide:
If to her share some female errors fall,
Look on her face, and you'll forget 'em all.

4
I am made to sow the thistle for wheat; the
    nettle for a nourishing dainty
I have planted a false oath in the earth, it has
    brought forth a poison tree
I have chosen the serpent for a councellor &
    the dog

For a schoolmaster to my children
I have blotted out from light & living the dove &
    nightingale
And I have caused the earth worm to beg from
    door to door
I have taught the thief a secret path into the
    house of the just
I have taught pale artifice to spread his nets upon
    the morning
My heavens are brass my earth is iron my moon a
    clod of clay
My sun a pestilence burning at noon & a vapour
    of death in night

What is the price of Experience do men buy it
    for a song
Or wisdom for a dance in the street? No it is
    bought with the price
Of all that a man hath his house his wife his
    children
Wisdom is sold in the desolate market where
    none come to buy
And in the witherd field where the farmer plows
    for bread in vain

5

Dust as we are, the immortal spirit grows
Like harmony in music; there is a dark
Inscrutable workmanship that reconciles
Discordant elements, makes them cling together
In one society. How strange that all
The terrors, pains, and early miseries,
Regrets, vexations, lassitudes interfused
Within my mind, should e'er have borne a part,
And that a needful part, in making up
The calm existence that is mine when I
Am worthy of myself! Praise to the end!
Thanks to the means which Nature deigned to
     employ;
Whether her fearless visitings, or those
That came with soft alarm, like hurtless light
Opening the peaceful clouds; or she may use
Severer interventions, ministry
More palpable, as best might suit her aim.

6

The woods decay, the woods decay and fall,
The vapours weep their burthen to the ground,
Man comes and tills the field and lies beneath,
And after many a summer dies the swan.
Me only cruel immortality

Consumes: I wither slowly in thine arms,
Here at the quiet limit of the world,
A white-haired shadow roaming like a dream
The ever-silent spaces of the East,
Far-folded mists, and gleaming halls of morn.

7

Yet each to keep and all, retrievements out of
    the night,
The song, the wondrous chant of the gray-brown
    bird,
And the tallying chant, the echo arous'd in
    my soul,
With the lustrous and drooping star with the
    countenance full of woe,
With the holders holding my hand nearing the
    call of the bird,
Comrades mine and I in the midst, and their
    memory ever to keep, for the dead I loved
    so well,
For the sweetest, wisest soul of all my days and
    lands—and this for his dear sake,
Lilac and star and bird twined with the chant of
    my soul,
There in the fragrant pines and the cedars dusk
    and dim.

8

Everything that man esteems
Endures a moment or a day.
Love's pleasure drives his love away,
The painter's brush consumes his dreams;
The herald's cry, the soldier's tread
Exhaust his glory and his might:
Whatever flames upon the night
Man's own resinous heart has fed.

9

There would still remain the never-resting mind,
So that one would want to escape, come back
To what had been so long composed.
The imperfect is our paradise.
Note that, in this bitterness, delight,
Since the imperfect is so hot in us,
Lies in flawed words and stubborn sounds.

We hear nine voices, all piercingly eloquent, and all making a difference to our consciousness that really is a difference. The first passage's speaker, Claudio, in Shakespeare's *Measure for Measure* (III, I, 117–131), faces execution, but while his cowardice (to call it that) is his own, there is nothing in his eloquence that reflects his individual consciousness. Instead, Shakespeare touches the universal with one of what we may call his own voices: our fear of death scarcely could be more vividly expressed.

In the next passage, the fallen angel Belial, in Milton's grand Debate in Hell (*Paradise Lost,* II, 145–151), may be echoing Claudio's lament as he too fears extinction. Is this one of Milton's own accents? Anything but a coward, the heroic, blind poet nevertheless allows Belial to catch a trace of the poet's own dread of being ended before his great poem had been fully composed.

With the third excerpt, we hear the exquisitely precise and modulated voice of Alexander Pope (*The Rape of the Lock,* Canto II, 1–18). The gorgeous Belinda, universal flirt, is aptly portrayed as a sunrise, warm to all but partial to none in particular. The Popean wit, Mozartean in its classical playfulness, achieves apotheosis in a couplet that commends itself to everyone:

> On her white breast a sparkling cross she wore,
> Which Jews might kiss, and infidels adore.

Pope's perfect pitch is answered by William Blake's prophetic tonalities in the fourth passage, the lament of Enion, the Earth Mother, in *The Four Zoas* (Night II,

p. 35, 1–15). In the accents of Zechariah 8:17 and Job 28:12–13, Blake speaks also in his own most authentic voice, as he himself is both seller and farmer:

> Wisdom is sold in the desolate market where
>   none come to buy
> And in the witherd field where the farmer plows
>   for bread in vain

A different prophet, William Wordsworth, is heard in (5), from *The Prelude* I, 340–356, where Nature is exalted as subtlest of poetic teachers. The profound melancholia of Tennyson's Vergilian "Tithonus" sounds in (6), a lament for an immortality rendered useless by perpetual aging. Prophecy returns in (7), with the final lines of Walt Whitman's "When Lilacs Last in the Dooryard Bloom'd," where Whitman's elegiac, rocking threnody achieves a deep peace.

William Butler Yeats, his voice at its most oracular, is heard in (8), the final stanza of his "Two Songs from a Play," with its paradox beyond bitterness: "love's pleasure drives his love away." A final contrast is afforded by (9), where Wallace Stevens concludes his subtle "The Poems of Our Climate" with the somber realization: "The imperfect is our paradise." Yeats's voice is fierce, but Stevens's is very quiet, as he is the poet who listens for and somehow renders what lies beyond representation, "The hum of thoughts evaded in the mind."

6

WHAT MAKES one poem better than another? The question, always central to the art of reading poetry, is more crucial today than ever before, since extrapoetic considerations of race, ethnicity, gender, sexual orientation, and assorted ideologies increasingly constitute the grounds for judgment in the educational institutions and the media of the English-speaking world.

One of the few gains from aging, at least for a critic of poetry, is that taste matures even as knowledge increases. As a younger critic, I tended to give my heart to the poetry of the Romantic tradition, doubtless spurred to polemics on its behalf by the distortions it suffered at the hands of T. S. Eliot and his New Critical academic followers: R. P. Blackmur, Allen Tate, Cleanth Brooks, W. K. Wimsatt among them. In my early seventies, I remain profoundly attached to the sequence that goes from Spenser through Milton on to the High Romantics (Blake, Wordsworth, Shelley, Keats) and then to the continuators in Tennyson, Browning, Whitman, Dickinson, Yeats, Stevens, Lawrence, Hart Crane. With Chaucer and Shakespeare, these remain the poets I love best, but maturation has brought an almost equal regard for the tradition of Wit: Donne, Ben Jonson, Marvell, Dryden, Pope, Byron, and such modern descendants as Auden and Eliot (a secret Romantic, however).

I juxtapose two short poems, one of which is bad indeed, the other superb.

Alone

From childhood's hour I have not been
As others were—I have not seen
As others saw—I could not bring
My passions from a common spring—
From the same source I have not taken
My sorrow—I could not awaken
My heart to joy at the same tone—
And all I lov'd—*I* lov'd alone—
Then—in my childhood—in the dawn
Of a most stormy life—was drawn
From ev'ry depth of good and ill

The mystery which binds me still—
From the torrent, or the fountain—
From the red cliff of the mountain—
From the sun that 'round me rolled
In its autumn tint of gold—
From the lightning in the sky
As it pass'd me flying by—
From the thunder, and the storm—
And the cloud that took the form
(When the rest of Heaven was blue)
Of a demon in my view—

The Rhodora

On Being Asked, Whence Is the Flower?

In May, when sea-winds pierced our solitudes,
I found the fresh Rhodora in the woods,
Spreading its leafless blooms in a damp nook,
To please the desert and the sluggish brook.
The purple petals, fallen in the pool,
Made the black water with their beauty gay;
Here might the red-bird come his plumes to
    cool,

And court the flower that cheapens his array.
Rhodora! if the sages ask thee why
This charm is wasted on the earth and sky,
Tell them, dear, that if eyes were made for
   seeing,
Then Beauty is its own excuse for being:
Why thou wert there, O rival of the rose!
I never thought to ask, I never knew;
But, in my simple ignorance, suppose
The self-same Power that brought me there
   brought you.

Both are poems by Americans in the mid-nineteenth century, each better known for his other writings. The first, "Alone," is palpably Byronic, and closely imitates the noble lord's self-portrait in his *Lara:*

There was in him a vital scorn of all:
As if the worst had fallen which could befall,
He stood a stranger in this breathing world,
An erring spirit from another hurled;
A thing of dark imaginings, that shaped
By choice the perils he by chance escaped;
But 'scaped in vain, for in their memory yet
His mind would half exult and half regret.

With more capacity for love than earth
Bestows on most of mortal mould and birth,
His early dreams of good outstripped the truth,
And troubled manhood followed baffled youth;
With thought of years in phantom chase
    misspent,
And wasted powers for better purpose lent;
And fiery passions that had poured their wrath
In hurried desolation o'er his path,
And left the better feelings all at strife
In wild reflection o'er his stormy life;

Byron's narcissism is smooth and self-delighting; his disciple, Edgar Allan Poe, is self-pitying and metrically maladroit, and reminds us that Ralph Waldo Emerson called him "the jingle man." Both *Lara* and "Alone" are melodramatic, but Byron has the aristocratic flair to bring it off, while Poe's litany of "I"s and "my"s is pathetic in the context of torrent and fountain, cliff and mountain, rolling sun and flying lightning, thunder and storm and cloud. By the time Poe sees a demon in the cloud, the reader is wearied.

Poe's antithesis, Emerson, in "The Rhodora," declines to answer the question: "Whence is the Flower?" He does not know why this beautiful "rival of the rose" is placed so inexplicably. With Poe, because of the derivative echoes, we are compelled to remember Byron. With Emerson, a reader of Robert Frost will think of Frost, Emerson's professed disciple. Frost's powerful "The Wood-Pile" and "The Oven Bird" follow the pattern of "The Rhodora," where natural beauty wastes without purpose.

Emerson, with his tough sensibility, too easily can be misread. The only God that Emerson knew was a God within the self, and so the Power of the final line cannot be identified with a benign, external God. Out of context, "Beauty is its own excuse for being" could be confused with the Aestheticism of Oscar Wilde. But in the poem, the line means that beauty is a throwaway, as the wood-walking Emerson may be also, so far as the Power or Fate is concerned.

The diction in "The Rhodora" is assured and confident, and its figurative stance approaches an ironic edge, over which Emerson declines to cross. His "simple ignorance" wants to be taken literally, but "The Rhodora" is too adroit for that.

There *are* a few good poems by Poe, but they too are derivative. "Israfel" is haunted by Shelley's "To a Skylark," while "The City in the Sea" rewrites Byron's "Darkness." How can one tell the difference between involuntary echoing and controlled allusiveness? That is a difficult question to answer, since only the cumulative experience of reading poetry could render a reply accessible.

Sometimes a poet will show his awareness of an allusion through the process of revision. Here are the two versions of the first stanza of Edwin Arlington Robinson's superb incantation "Luke Havergal":

> Go to the western gate, Luke Havergal,—
> There where the vines cling crimson on the
>   wall,—
> And in the twilight wait for what will come.
> The wind will moan, the leaves will whisper
>   some—
> Whisper of her, and strike you as they fall;
> But go, and if you trust her she will call.
> Go to the western gate, Luke Havergal—
> Luke Havergal.

> Go to the western gate, Luke Havergal,
> There where the vines cling crimson on the wall,
> And in the twilight wait for what will come.
> The leaves will whisper there of her, and some,
> Like flying words, will strike you as they fall;

But go, and if you listen she will call.
Go to the western gate, Luke Havergal—
Luke Havergal.

The modification is from: "The wind will moan,
the leaves will whisper some— / Whisper of her, and
strike you as they fall" to: "The leaves will whisper
there of her, and some, / Like flying words, will strike
you as they fall." Certainly the second version is even
more eloquent, and the allusion to Shelley's "Ode to
the West Wind" is rendered unmistakable. Shelley's
figuration, in which dead leaves and words fuse, kin-
dles Robinson's revision:

Drive my dead thoughts over the universe
Like withered leaves to quicken a new birth!
And, by the incantation of this verse,

Scatter, as from an unextinguished hearth
Ashes and sparks, my words among mankind!

Where are the flying words in Robinson's poem?
"Trust" is altered to "listen" in the next line, and at the
poem's conclusion the leaves are "dead words." Robin-
son strengthens his poem by making the allusion

clearer. This dramatic lyric is chanted by Luke Havergal, rather than by Robinson, which helps the poet transmute Shelley's prophetic outcry into a highly individual litany for lost love.

The poetic excellence of "Luke Havergal" partly ensues from rhetorical control, the verbal equivalent of personal self-confidence. A faltering of voice mars, and can destroy, any poem whatsoever. Sustained and justified pride of performance is a frequent attribute of the best lyric poetry. Generally it is more appropriate that the pride be implicit, but there is a particular pleasure for the attentive reader when a poet justifies self-referentiality as Shelley does in the fifty-fifth and final stanza of *Adonais*, his elegy for John Keats:

> The breath whose might I have invoked in song
> Descends on me; my spirit's bark is driven,
> Far from the shore, far from the trembling
> throng
> Whose sails were never to the tempest given;
> The massy earth and spherèd skies are riven!
>
> I am borne darkly, fearfully, afar;
> Whilst, burning through the inmost veil of
> Heaven,

> The soul of Adonais, like a star,
> Beacons from the abode where the Eternal are.

Shelley welcomes the "destroyer and preserver" invoked in his own "Ode to the West Wind," which now powers his spirit (breath) for a final, cosmological voyage. To thus call upon a prior creation of one's own is to affirm an authentic poetic election. Keats, wonderfully pugnacious by temperament, confronts his fierce Muse, Moneta, in *The Fall of Hyperion,* and proudly emphasizes his solitary election:

> I sure should see
> Other men here; but I am here alone.

The preternatural confidence of poetic election is unsurpassed in Walt Whitman, who at the start of section 25, *Song of Myself,* achieves apotheosis:

> Dazzling and tremendous how quick the sun-rise
>   would kill me,
> If I could not now and always send sun-rise out
>   of me.
>
> We also ascend dazzling and tremendous as
>   the sun,

> We found our own O my soul in the calm and
> cool of the day-break.

> My voice goes after what my eyes cannot reach,
> With the twirl of my tongue I encompass worlds
> and volumes of worlds.

The play upon "quick" is superb, since it means both "speed" and "life." A perpetual American sunrise, Walt Whitman here also alludes to Jehovah, who walks in the Garden of Eden before the heat of the day. What makes Whitman the best of all American poets—except for his one rival, Emily Dickinson—is harmonic balance. At his greatest, he is flawless, with no false notes. Who could improve even a single phrase of the concluding section of *Song of Myself* ?

> The spotted hawk swoops by and accuses me, he
> complains of my gab and my loitering.

> I too am not a bit tamed, I too am untranslatable,
> I sound my barbaric yawp over the roofs of the
> world.

> The last scud of day holds back for me,
> It flings my likeness after the rest and true as any

on the shadow'd wilds,
It coaxes me to the vapor and the dusk.

I depart as air, I shake my white locks at the
    runaway sun,
I effuse my flesh in eddies, and drift it in
    lacy jags.

I bequeath myself to the dirt to grow from the
    grass I love,
If you want me again look for me under your
    boot-soles.

You will hardly know who I am or what I mean,
But I shall be good health to you nevertheless,
And filter and fibre your blood.

Failing to fetch me at first keep encouraged,
Missing me one place search another,
I stop somewhere waiting for you.

There is nothing "free" about this verse: in measure
and phrase, it has that quality of the *inevitable* that is
central to great poetry. "Inevitable," in this context,
takes its primary meaning, phrasing that cannot be

avoided, that *must be,* rather than the secondary mean-
ing of "invariable" or "predictable." Indeed, the differ-
ence between those meanings is a pragmatic test for
distinguishing between the best poems and merely imi-
tative verses. "If you want me again look for me under
your boot-soles" is unavoidable wording, while Poe's "In
there stepped a stately Raven of the saintly days of yore"
is woefully predictable.

The two kinds of "inevitability" are also two modes
of the memorable. I can chant Poe by the yard, from
memory, because it is jack-in-the-box verse, mechanical
and repetitive. But when I possess a great poem by
memory, it is because the work is inevitable, perfectly
fulfilled and fulfillable. In the better mode of the mem-
orable, cognition is a vital element in possession. Thus,
I tend to recite Tennyson's superb dramatic monologue
"Ulysses" to myself, on days when I have to battle
depression or adversity, or just the consequences of old
age. Frequently, I ask classes to read and reread
"Ulysses" out loud to themselves while thinking and
rethinking it through. What could be more inevitable, in
the grand sense of what must be?

> There lies the port; the vessel puffs her sail:
> There gloom the dark broad seas. My mariners,

Souls that have toiled, and wrought, and thought
    with me—
That ever with a frolic welcome took
The thunder and the sunshine, and opposed
Free hearts, free foreheads—you and I are old;
Old age hath yet his honour and his toil;
Death closes all: but something ere the end,
Some work of noble note, may yet be done,
Not unbecoming men that strove with Gods.
The lights begin to twinkle from the rocks:
The long day wanes: the slow moon climbs: the
    deep
Moans round with many voices. Come, my
    friends,
'Tis not too late to seek a newer world.
Push off, and sitting well in order smite
The sounding furrows; for my purpose holds
To sail beyond the sunset, and the baths
Of all the western stars, until I die.
It may be that the gulfs will wash us down:
It may be we shall touch the Happy Isles,
And see the great Achilles, whom we knew.
Though much is taken, much abides; and though
We are not now that strength which in old days
Moved earth and heaven; that which we are,
    we are;

One equal temper of heroic hearts,
Made weak by time and fate, but strong in will
To strive, to seek, to find, and not to yield.

"Though much is taken, much abides": that seems to me the essence of positive inevitability of phrasing. When Ben Jonson remarked bitterly of Shakespeare, "He never blotted a line—would he had blotted many!," he testified to Shakespeare's uncanny power of unavoidable rather than predictable phrasing. Tennyson's Ulysses is overtly Shakespearean throughout his monologue, until in the final lines he begins to sound like Milton's quite Shakespearean Satan. In Shakespeare, more than in any other poet in English, we continually receive the impression of a control over phrasemaking so great that everything in the mind that is out of control finds itself organized by the inevitability of the power to phrase. John Keats, enraptured by this Shakespearean capability, seems to have associated it with Coleridge's Organic analogue, as when Keats observes that if a poem does not come as naturally as leaves to a tree, then it had better not come at all. The notion that Shakespeare and nature are everywhere the same is a false though poignant one. And yet that tribute to Shakespeare helps illuminate the idea of inevitability as unavoidable wording rather than merely predictable diction.

Matthew Arnold thought that this inevitability of great poetry could be clarified by the citation of "touchstones," brief passages of Homer, Dante, Shakespeare, and Milton against which other poems could be tested. But Arnold deliberately chose to be imprecise when he spoke of his touchstones as possessing "a high poetic stamp of diction and movement." That "movement" palpably is Arnold's own trope, as "inevitability" is mine, and does not illumine the question of how great poetry is to be recognized. A contrast of the true sense of "inevitability"—the unavoidable as opposed to the invariable—may take us closer to answering the question than the Arnoldian reliance upon the "movement" of touchstones, though *any* quotation from great poetry is bound to be a kind of touchstone, however we intend it.

The ancient idea of the Sublime, as set forth by the Hellenistic critic we call "Longinus," seems to me the origin of my expectation that great poetry will possess an inevitability of phrasing. Longinus tells us that in the experience of the Sublime we apprehend a greatness to which we respond by a desire for identification, so that we will become what we behold. Loftiness is a quality that emanates from the realm of aspiration, from what Wordsworth called a sense of something evermore *about to be.*

7

"INEVITABILITY," unavoidable phrasing, seems to me, then, a crucial attribute of great poetry. But how can a reader tell, for herself, whether a poem she has never seen before possesses the quality of authentic poetry? As you read a poem, there should be several questions in your mind. What does it mean, and how is that meaning attained? Can I judge how good it is? Has it transcended the history of its own time and the events of the poet's life, or is it now only a period piece?

I want to take as test case one of the great but truly difficult poems of the twentieth century, Hart Crane's *Voyages* II:

> —And yet this great wink of eternity,
> Of rimless floods, unfettered leewardings,
> Samite sheeted and processioned where
> Her undinal vast belly moonward bends,
> Laughing the wrapt inflections of our love;
>
> Take this Sea, whose diapason knells
> On scrolls of silver snowy sentences,
> The sceptered terror of whose sessions rends
> As her demeanors motion well or ill,
> All but the pieties of lovers' hands.

And onward, as bells off San Salvador
Salute the crocus lustres of the stars,
In these poinsettia meadows of her tides,—
Adagios of islands, O my Prodigal,
Complete the dark confessions her veins spell.

Mark how her turning shoulders wind the hours,
And hasten while her penniless rich palms
Pass superscription of bent foam and wave,—
Hasten, while they are true,—sleep, death,
    desire,
Close round one instant in one floating flower.

Bind us in time, O Seasons clear, and awe.
O minstrel galleons of Carib fire,
Bequeath us to no earthly shore until
Is answered in the vortex of our grave
The seal's wide spindrift gaze toward paradise.

The first draft of this visionary lyric was begun in
April 1924, three months away from Hart Crane's
twenty-fifth birthday, and in the early ecstatic phase of
his love for a Danish sailor, Emil Oppfer. This second
Voyage is part of a sequence of six. Let us commence
with a very close reading of Hart Crane's lyric, before

considering its contexts in Crane's life and works, and in the poetic tradition he accepted and sought to extend: Shakespeare, Marlowe, Blake, Shelley, Melville, Whitman, Dickinson, and his immediate precursor, the early T. S. Eliot, with whose work he had an agonistic relationship, as I think Wallace Stevens and William Carlos Williams did also.

The *Voyages* are poems of intense erotic fulfillment set in the Caribbean, where Crane had sojourned in summertime, with his grandmother, on the Isle of Pines, since he was fifteen. At thirty-two, returning to New York City from a Guggenheim year in Mexico City, Crane drowned himself in the Caribbean, but *Voyages* II was composed seven years before. "Sleep, death, desire / Close round one instant in one floating flower" has taken on, for some, the authority of prophecy.

The initial line: "—And yet this great wink of eternity" plays against the final line of *Voyages* I: "The bottom of the sea is cruel." Whether we are to find flirtation in the Caribbean's wink is unclear; it is, after all, a signal from eternity, ordinarily hardly an erotic possibility. John Keats had said to his silent Grecian urn that it teased us out of thought, as did eternity. Yet for Hart Crane the great wink emanates from a maternal sea that is at least equivocal, if not invasive, in regard to

the young men who have become lovers. Floods with
no rim or horizon, leewardings wholly free, as though
the wind's direction were open forever; these intimate
an available female presence beyond flirtation, danger-
ous because she incarnates the Oedipal trespass.
Sheeted in samite, the medieval rich, golden, silk gar-
ment of Tennysonian temptresses, the Caribbean
passes by as in an undine's procession. The sea's swell,
bending upward to the moon's pull, is the vast belly of a
water demoness in search of a soul. Ambiguously
maternal, does she laugh with or at the young men's
"wrapt inflections"? Crane, by "inflections," appears to
mean "motions," the rival "bendings" of the young
men, rather than any pitch of voice, in love's expres-
sion. "Wrapt," a Lewis Carrollian or Joycean portman-
teau word, pertains to rapt embraces yet also to the
sea's wrapping, the context through which the lovers
sail.

At fifteen, Hart Crane had read Shelley, and two
poems seem to have lingered in him: the early quest-
vision, *Alastor,* and the late elegy for Keats, *Adonais.*
Alastor evidently suggested the voyage motif to
Crane, while *Adonais* inspired the rhapsodic
"Atlantis" canto of Crane's epic, *The Bridge,* where
Atlantis is stationed last but was the first section of

the poem to be composed. *Alastor* was written when the twenty-three-year-old Shelley mistakenly thought he was dying of consumption. His friend, the ironic novelist Thomas Love Peacock (*Nightmare Abbey, Headlong Hall*) said that he restored the young, vegetarian poet to health by feeding him a steady diet of well-peppered muttonchops. Before this Peacockian firming-up, Shelley had sent his surrogate, a nameless young poet, upon a vast wandering through the ruins of the ancient world, and into an erotic quasi-dream union with a mysterious beauty in the "vale of Cashmir" (now much disputed between India and Pakistan). After the lady vanishes, the Poet searches for her, eventually sailing off in a little shallop upon what appears to be the Black Sea, which Shelley associated with death, night, and the mothering aspect of nature.

Shelley thus inaugurated what would become more an American than an English poetic motif, the fourfold figuration that finally fuses night, death, the mother, and the sea in a sequence of American poets from Walt Whitman though Hart Crane, Wallace Stevens, T. S. Eliot, and beyond. Losing the visionary beloved, Shelley's Poet laments the mutual spell of sleep, death, desire:

>   Alas! Alas!
> Were limbs, and breath, and being indetermined
> Thus treacherously? Lost, lost, forever lost,
> In the wide pathless desert of dim sleep,
> That beautiful shape? Does the dark gate of
>   death
> Conduct to thy mysterious paradise,
> O Sleep? Does the bright arch of rainbow clouds,
> And pendent mountains seen in the calm lake,
> Lead only to a black and watery depth,
> While death's blue vault, with loathliest vapours
>   hung
> Where every shade which the foul grave exhales
> Hides its dead eye from the detested days,
> Conducts, O Sleep, to thy delightful realms?

This deliciously unhealthy passage surprisingly makes death the gate to an erotic paradise of dream in sleep, a variant upon Hamlet's soliloquy that meditates upon the "sleep of death." Behind Shelley's speculation, as Crane seems to have known, perhaps through reading P. D. Ouspensky's *Tertium Organum* in 1923, was the Hellenistic myth of Hermes Trismegistus, reputed author of the *Poimandres,* where Divine Man falls into the ocean that is the cosmos of love, sleep, and death:

When the man saw in the water the form like
himself as it was in nature, he loved it and
wished to inhabit it; wish and action came in
the same moment, and he inhabited the
unreasoning form. Nature took hold of her
beloved, hugged him all about and embraced
him, for they were lovers.

. . . although man is above the cosmic
framework, he became a slave within
it . . . love and sleep are his masters.

—TRANS. B. P. COPENHAVEN

Like the Hermetic and Shelleyan falls into love and
sleep, Crane's lovers are knowingly narcissistic, and the
mockingly maternal sea punishes them for it. "Take this
Sea," Crane cries to his lover, and it is difficult to mark
the limits of that "take." In a poem so initially intense as
this, it almost seems as though Crane invites Oppfer to
join him in the act of Oedipal violation. If the undinal
vast mother is being embraced, all her attributes are
menacing. Her diapason, the full range of her outpour-
ing sound, *knells* (proclaims by the tolling of bells) on
the scrolls of silver snowy sentences, the Caribbean's
shifting surfaces, and "sentences" must mean court
judgments as well as the lines of *Voyages* II, a reading
confirmed by the brilliant "The sceptred terror of her

sessions *rends,*" a hint of an Orphic *sparagmos* that she could willfully inflict, depending upon our interpretation of her ambiguous countenance and its ambivalent gestures. There is a wonderful pathos in "all but the pieties of lovers' hands," but that sets the question of how we are to visualize the lovers. Do they hold hands in a Shelleyan boat, braving the Caribbean, or are we to see them as afloat, hand in hand, carried by the sea itself?

Though we must not literalize this superbly organized procession of images, both visualizations are possible, the boat voyage, of course, likelier. The third stanza exemplifies this: Crane and Oppfer sail onward, hearing a different voice of bells, whether of a sunken city or of long-submerged Spanish galleons, and these bells *salute* both sky and sea as visions of fresh growth, crocus lustres, and poinsettia meadows. In an ecstasy of sexual knowing, Crane cries aloud with preternatural eloquence:

> Adagios of islands, O my Prodigal,
> Complete the dark confessions her veins spell.

To salute Oppfer as "my Prodigal" is overtly Whitmanian, taking the beloved comrade not as extravagantly wasteful but as one who gives in abundance, with homoerotic profusion of being. Crane himself explained "Adagios of islands" as the slow, rocking motion a small boat made as it sailed though closely arrayed islets. It is not clear whether "adagios" refers to a slow musical movement or a deliberate *pas de deux,* here erotic, because of the passionate reference to the closing lines of section 21 of *Song of Myself,* where Whitman proclaims:

> Prodigal, you have given me love—
>   therefore I to you give love!
> O unspeakable passionate love.

Directly after, at the start of section 22, Whitman erotically encounters the sea:

> You Sea! I resign myself to you also—I guess
>   what you mean,
> I behold from the beach your crooked inviting
>   fingers,
> I believe you refuse to go back without feeling of
>   me,
> We must have a turn together, I undress, hurry
>   me out of sight of the land,

Cushion me soft, rock me in billowy drowse,
Dash me with amorous wet, I can repay you.

There is no overt anxiety here, or in Whitman's Oedipal trespass in "When Lilacs Last in the Dooryard Bloom'd":

> Dark mother always gliding near with soft feet,
> Have none chanted for thee a chant of fullest
>   welcome?
> Then I chant it for thee, I glorify thee above all,
> I bring thee a song that when thou must indeed
>   come, come unfalteringly.
>
> Approach strong deliveress,
> When it is so, when thou hast taken them I
>   joyously sing the dead,
> Lost in the loving floating ocean of thee,
> Laved in the flood of thy bliss O death.

Crane's mother-sea, the Caribbean, is far more equivocal in what seems to be the joined passion of the male lovers and the undine, where the homoerotic adagios "Complete the dark confessions her veins spell." But whose confessions are these?

The sea holds the sceptre, and the confessions are those of the lovers, under her spell, but also spelled by her veins (imagistically, foam) in the sentences of her scrolls. Certainly, the ambivalently maternal sea is again the center in the fourth stanza:

> Mark how her turning shoulders wind the hours,
> And hasten while her penniless rich palms
> Pass superscription of bent foam and wave,—
> Hasten, while they are true,—sleep, death,
>   desire,
> Close round one instant in one floating flower.

A superscription is something written above or inside something else. But to pass superscription is to make such writing into another judgmental sentence, and here the term set is time itself. The sea's turning shoulders form a timepiece, and Crane urges his lover to mark this in a double sense: to notice and to indicate for memory. The "penniless rich palms" are the mother's, awarding nothing and everything, and they are also palm trees floating in the "bent foam and wave." Crane, who makes even his syntax figurative, does not clarify the antecedent of "they" in "Hasten while they are true." Are they the sea's palms or, more likely, "sleep, death, desire"? As in

Shelley or in Hermetic writing, we fall into the narcissistic mirror of the sea, and sleep, death, and love fuse together. "Hasten" means to abandon the adagio phase of lovemaking, so as to achieve culmination: "Close round one instant in one floating flower," which may imply that what Shelley called "the boat of my desire" is now both exalted and reduced to the state of palm fronds floating in the sea. If the boat is still there, it is very frail indeed, and pragmatically voyaging has been transformed into floating in the sea:

> Bind us in time, O Seasons clear, and awe.
> O minstrel galleons of Carib fire,
> Bequeath us to no earthly shore until
> Is answered in the vortex of our grave
> The seal's wide spindrift gaze toward paradise.

The guiding genius of the poem here at the close is Melville rather than Whitman, and the end of Captain Ahab's voyage haunts the conclusion of Crane's and Oppfer's. "The seal's wide spindrift [which is windblown sea spray] gaze toward paradise" has a yearning for the mother in it, recalling the young seals who, in Chapter 126 of *Moby-Dick*, cry out because they have become separated from their dams. As Ahab goes on to his doom, "lovely leewardings" are associated with "something else than common land, more palmy than the palms." William Blake is also invoked in this ultimate stanza, since the "vortex of our graves" refers to his conceptual image of the "vortex," which closes the perceptual gap between subject and object.

Crane prays to "Seasons clear, and awe," probably in Emily Dickinson's sense of "awe," the name she gave to her love for Judge Otis Lord, and which she associated with Eternity. The prayer to be covenanted or bound in time, and the "minstrel galleons of Carib fire" may go back to the bells off San Salvador. The prayer is suicidal, prophesying Crane's leap into the Caribbean seven years later, since the bodies of the lovers are not to be washed ashore until the seal's longing gaze for the lost mother is answered "in the vortex of our grave," which in the Blakean sense of vortex intimates a resurrection, in which subject and object, spirit and body, unite again. And yet the tonalities of this concluding stanza are not suicidal, because desire is exalted over sleep and death. "Bind us" remains the dominant yearning, and the celebration of erotic completion continues to be ecstatic.

Voyages II revels in an absolute cognitive music, making enormous demands upon me, which it justifies by what I have termed "inevitability" in phrasing, measure, and rhythm. Like Coleridge's "Kubla Khan" and Keats's Great Odes, Crane's supreme lyric binds us both in and out of time.

8

HART CRANE is a difficult great poet, but very good, even great, poetry need not be overtly difficult. A. E. Housman is a clear instance, and there are many others. There are also difficult poets who at first look easy, but are not. Walt Whitman proclaims his accessibility, but his best poems are subtle, evasive, Hermetic, and call for a heightened awareness of the nuances of figuration.

Difficulty in great poetry can be of several, very different, kinds. Sustained allusiveness, as in the learned poetry of John Milton and Thomas Gray, demands a very high level of reader's literacy. Cognitive originality, the particular mark of Shakespeare and of Emily Dickinson, requires enormous intellectual agility as the reader's share. Personal mythmaking, as in William Blake and William Butler Yeats, at first can seem obscure, but the coherence of Blakean and Yeatsian myth yields to familiarity.

I think that poetry at its greatest—in Dante, Shakespeare, Donne, Milton, Blake—has one broad and essential difficulty: it is the true mode for expanding our consciousness. This it accomplishes by what I have learned to call *strangeness*. Owen Barfield was one of several critics to bring forth *strangeness* as a poetic criterion. For him, as for Walter Pater before him, the Romantic added strangeness to beauty: Wallace Stevens, a part of this tradition, has a Paterian figure cry out: "And there I found myself more truly and more strange." Barfield says: "It must be a strangeness of *meaning*," and then makes a fine distinction:

> It is not correlative with wonder; for wonder is our reaction to things which we are conscious of not quite understanding, or at any rate of understanding less than we had thought. The element of strangeness in beauty has the contrary effect. It arises from contact with a different kind of *consciousness* from our own, different, yet not so remote that we cannot partly share it, as indeed, in such a connection, the mere word "contact" implies. Strangeness, in fact, arouses wonder when we do not understand: aesthetic imagination when we do.

Consciousness is the central term here. As Barfield intimates, consciousness is to poetry what marble is to sculpture: the material that is being worked. Words are figurations of consciousness: metaphorical of consciousness, the poet's words invite us to share in a strangeness. "A felt change in consciousness" is one of Barfield's definitions of the poetic effect, and I relate this to what fascinates me most in the greatest Shakespearean characters—Falstaff, Hamlet, Iago, Lear, Cleopatra— the extraordinary changes that come about when they *overhear* themselves. As James Wood remarks, actually they become conscious of listening to Shakespeare, because in overhearing themselves, what they are hearing is Shakespeare. They become themselves more truly and more strange, because they are "free artists of themselves" (Hegel's tribute to them).

The work of great poetry is to aid *us* to become free artists of ourselves. Even Shakespeare cannot make me into Falstaff or Hamlet, but all great poetry asks us to be possessed by it. To possess it by memory is a start, and to augment our consciousness is the goal. The art of reading poetry is an authentic training in the augmentation of consciousness, perhaps the most authentic of healthy modes.

RECOMMENDED READING

GEOFFREY CHAUCER
   from The Canterbury Tales
   The General Prologue
   The Wife of Bath's Prologue
   The Pardoner's Prologue

WILLIAM DUNBAR
   Lament for the Makers

SIR THOMAS WYATT
   Whoso List to Hunt
   They Flee from Me

SIR PHILIP SIDNEY
Astrophel and Stella

EDMUND SPENSER
The Faerie Queene: The Gardens of Adonis
Epithalamion
Prothalamion

SIR WALTER RALEGH
The Ocean to Cynthia
Answer to Marlowe

CHIDIOCK TICHBORNE
Tichborne's Elegy

ROBERT SOUTHWELL
The Burning Babe

CHRISTOPHER MARLOWE
Tamburlaine
The Passionate Shepherd to His Love

MICHAEL DRAYTON
Idea

WILLIAM SHAKESPEARE

The Phoenix and Turtle

Hamlet

Troilus and Cressida

Measure for Measure

King Lear

The Tempest

Sonnets

XIX: "Devouring Time, blunt thou the lion's paws,"

XXX: "When to the sessions of sweet silent thought"

LIII: "What is your substance, whereof are you made,"

LV: "Not marble, nor the gilded monuments"

LXXIII: "That time of year thou mayst in me behold"

LXXXVI: "Was it the proud full sail of this great verse,"

LXXXVII: "Farewell—thou art too dear for my possessing,"

JOHN CLEVELAND
   Mark Antony

JAMES SHIRLEY
   Dirge

ROBERT HERRICK
   To the Virgins, To Make Much of Time
   Upon Julia's Clothes
   Delight in Disorder

THOMAS CAREW
   A Rapture
   Song

RICHARD LOVELACE
   La Bella Bona Roba
   Song
   To Althea, from Prison

SIR JOHN SUCKLING
   Song
   "Out upon it! I have loved"

HENRY VAUGHAN
>   Peace
>   The World
>   "They are all gone into the world of light!"
>   Cock-Crowing

THOMAS TRAHERNE
>   Shadows in the Water

JOHN MILTON
>   *Sonnets*
>>   XVII: "When I consider how my light is spent,"
>>   XVIII: "Avenge, O Lord, thy slaughtered saints,
>>   whose bones"
>>   XIX: "Methought I saw my late espousèd saint"
>   Lycidas
>   Paradise Lost
>   Samson Agonistes

JOHN DRYDEN
>   Religio Laici
>   To the Memory of Mr. Oldham
>   Lines on Milton

ROBERT BURNS

Address to the Deil

Holy Willie's Prayer

Scots Wha Hae

WILLIAM BLAKE

The Marriage of Heaven and Hell

Songs of Innocence and of Experience

The Sick Rose

The Tyger

Ah! Sun-flower

London

The Mental Traveller

The Crystal Cabinet

The Four Zoas

Milton

Jerusalem

The Gates of Paradise

WILLIAM WORDSWORTH

Tintern Abbey

Lines

The Lucy Poems

"Strange fits of passion have I known:"
"She dwelt among the untrodden ways"
"Three years she grew in sun and shower,"
"A slumber did my spirit seal;"
"I travelled among unknown men,"

Resolution and Independence
Ode: Intimations of Immortality from
    Recollections of Early Childhood
The Solitary Reaper
The Prelude

SAMUEL TAYLOR COLERIDGE
The Rime of the Ancient Mariner
Kubla Khan
Christabel
Dejection: An Ode

GEORGE GORDON, LORD BYRON
Childe Harold's Pilgrimage, A Romaunt
Don Juan
On This Day I Complete My Thirty-sixth Year

PERCY BYSSHE SHELLEY

Prometheus Unbound

Ode to the West Wind

The Two Spirits: An Allegory

Epipsychidion

Adonais

Hellas

With a Guitar, to Jane

Lines Written in the Bay of Lerici

The Triumph of Life

JOHN KEATS

On the Sea

La Belle Dame Sans Merci

Ode to Psyche

Ode to a Nightingale

Ode on a Grecian Urn

Ode on Melancholy

Hyperion

The Fall of Hyperion

To Autumn

Bright Star

This Living Hand

WILLIAM CULLEN BRYANT
  To a Waterfowl

RALPH WALDO EMERSON
  Uriel
  Ode, Inscribed to W. H. Channing
  Bacchus
  Days

HENRY WADSWORTH LONGFELLOW
  Snow-Flakes
  The Cross of Snow
  The Tide Rises, the Tide Falls
  The Bells of San Blas

EDGAR ALLAN POE
  Israfel
  The City in the Sea

JONES VERY
  The New Birth
  The Dead

HENRY DAVID THOREAU
  "My life has been the poem I would have writ,"

"I am a parcel of vain strivings tied"

"Light-winged Smoke, Icarian bird,"

JULIA WARD HOWE

Battle-Hymn of the Republic

WALT WHITMAN

Song of Myself

As Adam Early in the Morning

Crossing Brooklyn Ferry

"Out of the cradle endlessly rocking,"

"As I ebb'd with the ocean of life,"

When Lilacs Last in the Dooryard Bloom'd

The Last Invocation

HERMAN MELVILLE

The Portent

Fragments of a Lost Gnostic Poem of the 12th
Century

The Maldive Shark

EMILY DICKINSON

"There's a certain Slant of light,"

"I felt a Funeral, in my Brain,"

"From Blank to Blank—"

"After great pain, a formal feeling comes—"

"I started Early—Took my Dog—"

"This Consciousness that is aware"

"Our journey had advanced—"

"The Tint I cannot take—is best—"

"Because I could not stop for Death—"

"My Life had stood—a Loaded Gun—"

"A Light exists in Spring"

"Tell all the Truth but tell it slant—"

"In Winter in my Room"

"Because that you are going"

"A Pit—but Heaven over it—"

"By a departing light"

"I dwell in Possibility—"

"Through what transports of Patience"

"We grow accustomed to the Dark—"

"No man saw awe, nor to his house"

ALFRED, LORD TENNYSON

Mariana

The Eagle

Ulysses

Morte d'Arthur

from The Princess

  The Splendour Falls

  Tears, Idle Tears

In Memoriam A. H. H.

Maud: A Monodrama

Crossing the Bar

EDWARD FITZGERALD

The Rubáiyát of Omar Khayyám

ROBERT BROWNING

My Last Duchess

Fra Lippo Lippi

A Toccata of Galuppi's

"Childe Roland to the Dark Tower Came"

Andrea del Sarto

MATTHEW ARNOLD

Dover Beach

GEORGE MEREDITH
Modern Love

A Ballad of Past Meridian

RUDYARD KIPLING
The Vampire

The Way Through the Woods

WILLIAM BUTLER YEATS
The Song of Wandering Aengus

Adam's Curse

The Cold Heaven

The Second Coming

The Wild Swans at Coole

The Double Vision of Michael Robartes

LIONEL JOHNSON
The Dark Angel

ERNEST DOWSON
Non sum qualis eram bonae sub regno Cynarae

THOMAS HARDY
Neutral Tones

The Darkling Thrush

EDWARD THOMAS
>   Liberty
>   The Owl
>   The Gallows

ISAAC ROSENBERG
>   Returning, We Hear the Larks
>   A Worm Fed on the Heart of Corinth

EDWIN ARLINGTON ROBINSON
>   Luke Havergal
>   For a Dead Lady
>   Eros Turannos

STEPHEN CRANE
>   War Is Kind

TRUMBULL STICKNEY
>   Mnemosyne
>   Eride, V

ROBERT FROST
>   After Apple-Picking
>   The Wood-Pile
>   The Oven Bird

EZRA POUND
>A Pact
>
>Planh for the Young English King

ELINOR WYLIE
>Wild Peaches

H. D. (HILDA DOOLITTLE)
>Orchard
>
>Garden

ROBINSON JEFFERS
>Shine, Perishing Republic
>
>Apology for Bad Dreams

MARIANNE MOORE
>Marriage

T. S. (THOMAS STEARNS) ELIOT
>The Love Song of J. Alfred Prufrock
>
>Preludes
>
>La Figlia Che Piange
>
>The Waste Land

JOHN CROWE RANSOM

Here Lies a Lady

Captain Carpenter

Blue Girls

CONRAD AIKEN

Morning Song of Senlin

And in the Hanging Gardens

Sea Holly

Preludes for Memnon

EDNA ST. VINCENT MILLAY

"If I should learn, in some quite casual way,"

LOUISE BOGAN

Women

Men Loved Wholly Beyond Wisdom

JOHN BROOKS WHEELWRIGHT

Fish Food

Come Over and Help Us

LÉONIE ADAMS

April Mortality

The Horn

Grapes Making

Bell Tower

ALLEN TATE

Aeneas at Washington

The Mediterranean

HART CRANE

Repose of Rivers

Voyages

At Melville's Tomb

from The Bridge

   To Brooklyn Bridge

   The Tunnel

   Atlantis

The Broken Tower